Peace, Samoa, Peace

A Dark Day in Samoa's Fight for Freedom

PEACE, SAMOA, PEACE

A Dark Day in Samoa's Fight for Freedom

Daniel Pouesi

Illustrations by **Somnath Chatterjee**

Information for *Peace, Samoa, Peace* came mainly from Michael Field's book, *Mau: Samoa's Struggle for Freedom* and his series *Invincible Strangers*. Additional sources: *American Samoa: 100 Years Under the United States Flag*, J. Robert Shaffer, *The Making of Modern Samoa*, Malama Meleisea, *Samoan Proverbial Expressions*, Dr. E. Shultz, and *America's Providential History*, Mark A. Beliles & Stephen K. McDowell.

I've left out or condensed some events from Samoa's *Mau* Movement (passive resistance to New Zealand authority) and added Samoan proverbial expressions (in English) and a little dialogue to tell this important story. Illustrations of the *Mau* are based on photos and accounts from the time period—the 1920s. Special thanks to my beta readers—my sisters, Aliitasi I. Pouesi and Ruth Fou.

For my wife, June

Blessed is the nation whose God is Yahweh,
The people whom He has chosen for His own inheritance.
Psalm 33:12 (Legacy Standard Bible)

FOREWORD

Have you ever been told that something you deeply believe in is a lie? Or that a lie was actually the truth?

This is the journey Tama Folau faces in this story of truth, belief, and discovery by Daniel Pouesi.

When Tama's teacher claims that his father's homeland of Samoa is not a Christian nation, Tama reacts as any humiliated young person might: he loses his temper. Feeling betrayed, he struggles with his emotions until his wise Grandfather Logo steps in.

Grandfather Logo guides Tama through the powerful stories of their ancestors, showing him how they faced authority during Samoa's darkest days in their fight for freedom. Through these tales, Tama learns not just about the resilience of his people but also about finding strength and understanding in the face of adversity and misinformation.

Join Tama as he navigates the challenging waters of truth and lies, armed with the wisdom of his heritage and the strength of his convictions.

~ **J. Robert Shaffer**
Author *Samoa: A Historical Novel*

An Angry Boy

Eleven-year-old Tama Folau stormed down the hallway and flung his backpack onto the living room floor. "I hate her!" he screamed, kicking his bag. Pain seared his toes, and a loud "Ouch!" jolted Grandpa Logo awake. The old man bolted upright in his recliner, a remote control stuck between his fingers like a swollen cigar. "Temper, temper," he chided. His baseball cap shifted on his head when he settled back into his recliner.

Tama slumped on the carpet, kneading his toes. "Sorry, Papa. My teacher made me so angry. She said Samoa is *not* a Christian nation!"

"If this is how you acted, you proved her point," Papa replied.

Tama heaved a sigh. "But Papa, Samoa *is* Christian."

Papa nudged his cap upward. "The Samoa I come from is self-governed. That means it rules itself. I can't say the same about you."

"It's the Samoan in me," Tama replied curtly.

Papa chuckled. "Let me tell you about your ancestors, and namesake, Tamasese, who fought for Samoa's independence and how *they* acted."

Teacups and Spoons

On the street, a Harley Davidson rumbled past, its deep growl fading into the distance. Grandpa welcomed the silence. "Do you remember when God commanded Adam to rule over all of His creatures? That was a *mandate*. Adam was also to govern himself, but he failed. A man who cannot control himself can do evil things. So, God allowed men to rule others to protect society.

"In 1923, an international mandate appointed a New Zealander named George Richardson to govern Western Samoa. A military man with big ideas, Richardson said, 'Samoans are like children; I will be their father.' He gave Samoan chiefs, known as *Faipule,* the authority to enforce all kinds of rules."

"Like what, Papa?" Tama asked.

"Like how many teacups and spoons a family could own. A senior *faipule* took away a man's chiefly title because he refused to have his knives, forks and spoons inspected."

"Wow!" Tama said. "That's mean."

"That's not all," Papa said, removing his baseball cap.

Good Intentions

"Richardson had good intentions. He wanted to build clinics and schools. But he also wanted Samoans to give up certain things—like their beloved cricket."

"But Samoans love sports!" Tama said.

"Exactly," Papa nodded. "And Samoans loved to visit other villages in their long boats. Richardson thought these visits or *malaga* wasted resources. But Richardson, himself, went on extravagant *malaga*. And wherever he went, a group of young boys, like you, went along, waving New Zealand and Union Jack flags. Most of the boys paraded bare-chested because Richardson wanted to show how healthy they were under his watch."

Papa paused, gazing into the distance as if picturing the scene. "At the villages, chiefs welcomed Richardson with the usual, customary words of respect. 'We in our ignorance and humility turn to you for the light of your wisdom. We are the children; you are our father.'

"This pleased Richardson. Perhaps after hearing this kind of praise many times, Richardson came to believe he really *was* Samoa's father. But not all Samoans accepted Richardson's ideas. They continued to go on big *malaga* and exchange gifts and their fine mats."

Remember the Talune!

Papa leaned back in his recliner, a pensive glimmer in his eyes. "When Samoans were unhappy with Richardson, they recalled the *Talune*."

"What's the *Talune*?" Tama asked, his curiosity piqued.

"*Talune* was a New Zealand passenger and cargo ship. You see, when people travel from one country to another, they take along many things—plants, animals, new technology, and ideas. But sometimes, they introduce diseases—sometimes intentionally," Papa explained.

"In November 1918, the *Talune* sailed into Apia, Samoa's capital. Six passengers had the Spanish Influenza. Perhaps, as one source reported, the passengers were told to pretend they were fine—that it was just seasickness. Despite the risk, the New Zealand Administrator, Robert Logan, allowed the *Talune* to dock. The influenza hurtled through Samoa like a

wild tornado, wiping out nearly a quarter of its population. Vaimoso, a village near Apia, was among the first to feel the influenza's wrath.

"Vaimoso was home for one of Samoa's high chiefs, Tupua Tamasese Lealofi III. Like many Samoans, Tamasese remembered the *Talune* and the trouble it caused."

Rifles!

"Tamasese saw more trouble when Richardson's Marines marched through town with rifles over their shoulders.

"Can you just hear it?" Papa said, drumming his recliner's armrest with his fingers. "Their booted feet thudding on the tarred surface of Apia's Beach Road. Dressed in striking, khaki uniforms and pith helmets, the Marines soon became a familiar sight. Their awesome presence inspired fear. For Richardson, it was important to display power to maintain peace and order."

Papa shifted in his chair, his voice softening. "Tamasese also loved peace and order. And he imagined a Samoa governed by Samoan people. He had a round face, much like

yours. His hair, combed upward from his forehead, looked like
a cliff. Imagine him watching those uniformed men, their heels
stirring up a whiff of decayed *pulu* seeds. Imagine Tamasese
clutching his singlet, his mind swirling with anxious thoughts,
perhaps even bordering on panic. He survived the influenza.
Wise beyond his years, he probably wondered, 'What's next?'"

Model Village

Tama gripped the edge of the sofa, clutching his tee shirt. "What happened next?"

Papa cleared his throat. "You know, Samoans live in communal lands. Richardson believed that if Samoan men owned their own, private plots, they'd work harder and produce more crops. He also thought villages should be remodeled to use the land better. He wanted huts in rows with an open field in the middle, a church in one corner, a cinema in the other, a blacksmith's shop in the third and so on.

"Some high chiefs, like Faumuina of Lepea, loved Richardson's idea," Papa continued. "'Let's follow Richardson's plan,' he said. So he ordered his people's huts to be torn down. Mango and breadfruit trees which provided food and shade for families fell to steel axes. And workers ignored ancestral graves that marked family boundaries. The remodeling caused the villagers much grief. Tamasese's Vaimoso was next in line.

An Angry Pastor

"Tamasese did not want Vaimoso remodeled. Ignoring Richardson, he planted a hibiscus hedge on his property. But one man's hibiscus hedge can be another man's prickly bush. Tamasese's hedge rattled a pastor. The pastor complained to the government. 'That man's hedge is blocking my view and violating Richardson's plan.'

"Richardson ordered Tamasese to cut down his hedge. Tamasese pruned it instead."

Tama burst into a boisterous laughter. "Wow, Papa! Tamasese would not let anyone bully him, eh?"

"Well, yes. But that hedge cost him. At an unexpected hour, policemen surprised him. They clapped cuffs on his wrists and hauled him away. For Richardson, it was a daring move. 'Samoans will see that all people, titled or not, are equal under the law,' he said.

"He was wrong. Samoans may not have rioted or burned down things, but they were like a sleeping volcano with fire swirling beneath. Richardson banished Tamasese to the island of Savai'i. But no banishment could keep away a loving father. When Tamasese heard his child was sick, he crossed the hostile lava fields of Savai'i, borrowed a canoe and paddled home. Richardson's men arrested him. But they underestimated the strength of the Samoan will.

False Hope

"Tempers were about to snap like rubber bands stretched too thinly. Faumuina warned Richardson, 'My people are saying we have become a town of many thoughts.'

"Richardson tapped his lips with a forefinger, mildly amused. 'Your people also say, when a mistake has been made inland, it must be corrected at the seaside. New Zealand's Governor General Charles Fergusson is visiting soon. He and I are on the seaside.'

"Fergusson's arrival filled Samoans with hope. They organized sports, staged dances, drank *'ava* and presented traditional gifts. The *Fetu* boys chanted 'Samoa is a great country; I am going to make it a better one.'

"Fergusson basked in the tribute. 'Richardson is doing a fine job here,' he said. 'The troublemakers are the white traders and half-castes.'

"Fergusson had in mind a particular man—a wealthy, Swedish-Samoan merchant named Olaf Nelson. Like Tamasese, Nelson was a respected high chief. He believed Samoans could run their own affairs. Richardson disagreed. 'Samoans are a simple people. They need a lot of education before they can do the things we're doing.' This difference in beliefs turned Richardson and Nelson into bitter enemies."

Faithful Faipule

Tama leaned forward, fingers interlaced. Papa continued, his voice sounding increasingly disconcerting. "Though things weren't going as Richardson planned, he insisted he'd get his way."

Tama unclasped his fingers, mixed emotions surging through him. "Papa, did not all chiefs stand with Tamasese and Nelson?"

"Some did. Others, like some *Faipule*, sided with Richardson. When they visited New Zealand in 1925, they were dazzled by New Zealand's wealth. They declared, 'We want New Zealand to be Samoa's guardian.'

"Tamasese and Nelson wanted Samoa to be Samoa's guardian. Richardson believed they were not ready. The Samoans, he said, knew nothing of the Modern Age.

"When Nelson went to Australia to see his doctor, an urgent message from his workers followed him. *Please go to New Zealand and fight for us. Richardson is moving with his Remodeling Plan. We have been ordered to return to our villages. Two of your workers have been arrested. And treated badly.*

No Hope

"In October of 1926, Nelson, known as Ta'isi to
Samoans, returned with urgent news and called a meeting. A
crowd of two hundred and fifty gathered at a market hall at
night to hear him. Among them were a white trader named
Alfred Smyth and Chief of Police, Braisby, who jotted down
what was said in the meeting. Standing at the front, Nelson
announced, 'Minister Nosworthy is coming to Samoa. He
will hear us.'

"The news sparked a second, even larger meeting. This
time, over six hundred people attended. Tamasese joined
them. The atmosphere tensed as policemen surrounded the
building with batons. Nelson's courage instilled calmness as
he offered a prayer. Just then, a man strode across the room
with a letter from Richardson. It began, 'Warning to the
people of Samoa. I ask you to stop cooperating with the
Europeans in their matters which do not concern you.'

"Murmurs animated the crowd. Nelson raised his hand
for silence. 'Richardson has blocked our voice. He's trying to
stop Nosworthy from coming. If Nosworthy won't come, we
will go to him. We are the Citizens' Group.'

"Seven people walked out. Five of them, a reporter said,
worked for the government earning thousands of pounds."

Tama couldn't contain himself. "Papa, it looked like
Richardson had a plan—divide and conquer."

All Men Are Equal

For a while, Papa was silent. Outdoors, the hum of the late afternoon traffic sounded like a bad track to a horror movie. Tama furrowed his brow, eyes dimmed by apprehension. "Papa, if Fergusson didn't hear the Samoans, why would—"

"Nosworthy?" Papa finished. "Nelson and Tamasese never lost hope, even with dark clouds gathering over their beloved Samoa. They feared these storms might break into a war among their people. That would have been a cross too heavy for them to bear.

"In March of 1927, the Citizens' Group announced a new group—the Samoan League, also known as *Mau*, meaning 'Opinion.' The group's first declaration showed the kind of government it wanted. 'We believe that man's call from God is to help others no matter their status, race, color, or creed. We believe all men are equal in the eyes of God.'

"Your teacher probably does not know the words 'All men are equal in the eyes of God' is a moral truth that is uniquely Christian. That truth is foreign to Samoans. But Tamasese, Nelson and the *Mau* adopted it.

"Anyway, the *Mau* elected a man named Matautia Karauna to be its secretary. He was the son of a pastor. Karauna's decision to join the *Mau* ignited a fire that would change everything."

The Only Cure

For a while, Papa was silent. Tama waited patiently though every tense sinew in his body screamed, 'Please, Papa, don't stop now!'

Papa drew a deep breath. "Well, Nosworthy arrived in time to celebrate the King of England's birthday. The government held races at Apia Park. The *Mau* celebrated with sports, and Nelson hosted a lavish ball. When Nosworthy finally met with the *Mau* leaders, a crowd packed the grounds around the Colonial Administration building, eager to hear him. If there was a shimmer of hope, it fled the moment Nelson and Nosworthy came face to face. The two

men snapped at each other. 'You are trying to be Samoa's government!' Nosworthy screamed. 'Deportation is the only cure for your and your white friends' meddling.'

"When the meeting failed to meet his demands, Richardson banished *Mau* leaders. In a striking show of allegiance, Faumuina sided with the *Mau*. Richardson had him arrested for unpaid taxes. As police officers cuffed the chief and drove him to a small island call Apolima, they met a group of angry Samoans with axes. 'Calm down, men!' Faumuina implored. His plea might as well have fallen on plugged ears."

No Way Out

Papa drew his legs up into his recliner. It was a posture
Tama had seen many times, especially when Papa was
about to say something extra important. "A country without
God is like a boat without a rudder. It may float. But it has
no destination. Armed with a letter signed by many chiefs,
Nelson went to New Zealand hopeful for change. A special
committee heard him. However, the committee's insensitive
remarks—perhaps like your teacher's—dashed all hopes for
a resolution and created the perfect surf break for a deadly
swell.

"Back at Vaimoso, the *Mau* vowed to resist peacefully.
'We will stop sending our children to government schools.
We will not pay taxes. We will give only to the *Mau*.'"

"But Papa," Tama interjected. "Didn't Jesus say give to Caesar what is Caesar's and to God what is God's?"

Papa beamed with pride. "You're right! If you don't give Caesar his due, he might just take more. And, in 1927, that's exactly what happened. Richardson got a new law passed that gave him power to exile anyone. He used it to banish Nelson for five years and Smyth for three. It was clear then the government and the *Mau* were on a road to collision.

Marines and Warships

"Back in January of 1928, the streets of Apia were alive. The *Mau* protested with songs, bold and defiant. You could spot them easily with their colorful attire: purple turbans, blue *lavalava* marked by stark white stripes, and their singlets catching the wind.

They boycotted town stores owned by white folks. That got under Richardson's skin. He needed the tax money. So, he contacted New Zealand, 'Send two warships and a small force. That will end the *Mau*.'

"And sure enough, two warships—the *Dunedin* and *Diomede*—came slicing through the waters into Apia Harbor.

"When Marines stepped off, armed to the teeth with machine guns, rifles, and pistols, you could feel the tension spike. They weren't messing around, barreling into town on lorries, horns screaming. The Marines rounded up about 400 *Mau* and hauled them off to Vaimea Prison. But here's the thing – those prisoners? They were smiling and waving like they were going on a picnic. In a move Richardson did not expect, a 150 *Mau* turned themselves in. Vaimea was bursting at the seams. It couldn't hold them all. If Richardson thought the Samoans were rebellious children, what happened next probably convinced him the Samoans could play any man's game and play it better.

That Conceited Tamasese!

"At night, prisoners walked out to watch a movie or visit friends, daring the guards to shoot them. In the morning, they returned for free breakfast. Realizing the *Mau* had outfoxed him, Richardson ordered all prisoners released. 'But arrest that conceited Tamasese!'

"When Marines tried to nab Tamasese, *Mau* police intervened. No one dared to lay a finger on the chief. Richardson suffered another blow when the *Dunedin* and *Diomede* left. The *Mau* upped its antics, taunting Richardson with rude and abrasive songs."

"Wow, songs can be powerful!" Tama said

"You betcha," Papa nodded. "Like the old Samoan
saying goes, 'A rock crumbles, but words survive.'
Richardson pleaded with New Zealand to arrest Tamasese.
'He is a conceited man who wants to be King!'

"'Come back home!' New Zealand replied. 'We are
sending a replacement to fix your problem.'"

Silent Steve

A clock chime startled Tama out of a reverie. Papa chuckled giving his belly a whop. "The *Mau* didn't just sit still; they grew stronger. When Richardson's replacement, a Military Man named Stephen Allen, arrived, he didn't pay them much mind. '*Mau* inactive – so am I,' he telegraphed New Zealand. He enjoyed the sun and breeze. But the breeze portended a storm."

Papa's voice grew serious. "Real trouble began when police clubbed *Mau* members over some infraction. When Tamasese protested, Allen told his people, 'It's time to break up the *Mau*.'

"In November of 1928, things escalated. Allen's men raided Tamasese's home. Behind the house, a police officer drew a pistol on Tamasese. 'Go on, shoot me, shoot me!' Tamasese said. A crowd gathered. Tamasese raised his cuffed hands and called, 'Peace, Samoa, peace.'

"But Allen wouldn't have peace. He exiled Tamasese to New Zealand, chained to a ship bunk. Nelson saw Tamasese in passing. As Tamasese descended the ship's gangway, Nelson thought his friend looked distressed. The truth? Tamasese's body was wracked with fever. He feared he would die alone in a foreign prison.

A Beast Sleepeth

"New Zealand government officials visited Tamasese
in jail. Following Allen's suggestion, they offered to take
him on a tour thinking New Zealand's wealth would
make him forget the *Mau*. Nelson thought Tamasese was
tempted just as Jesus was. 'I am a prisoner,' Tamasese
said. 'I shall remain steadfast in the *Mau* of Samoa.'

"After six months in Mount Eden Jail, Tamasese
returned to Samoa. He wept for joy as he crossed from
the ship *Tofua* to the shore over long boats linked bow to
stern. Allen ordered the island newspaper not to write
about Tamasese's homecoming."

"Papa, that's suppression of the press!"

"Well, in Samoa, you can't suppress happiness.
Smoke billowed from the cooking huts as young men

fired up their stone ovens to prepare a feast. Dancers donned costumes and lit their fireknives, their faces alight with excitement, to welcome their hero. At the head of the parade, a village band strutted, its brass instruments gleaming in the sun. But amid the celebrations, trouble prowled in the shadows like a hungry beast."

The Beast Awaketh!

The hairs on the back of Tama's neck bristled. Papa could drum up some pretty scary Samoan *fagogo*. But this was no folktale.

"Remember Alfred Smyth?" Papa asked. "He was a friend of the *Mau*. When the *Mau* heard Smyth and a friend were returning to Samoa, they decided to throw another feast. Bullocks, pigs, and chickens were slaughtered by the score. Boatloads of freshly-harvested taro, breadfruit, yams, and green bananas were rowed in from Savaii, all to welcome Smyth with a feast fit for royalty.

"But the tension in the air was unmistakable," Papa continued, pausing for effect. "Allen sent Tamasese a warning. 'Any lawbreakers seen at your parade will be

arrested.' Allen had his sight on one man—Matautia Karauna—the pastor's son."

Papa's voice fell to a whisper. "Early Saturday morning, December 28, 1929, the schooner, *Lady Roberts,* moored off Apia Harbor. Seven hundred Samoans marched from Tamasese's Vaimoso to greet Smyth— another seven hundred from East of Apia. On that day, the beast stirred. Its shadow fell widely. Its purpose was to turn a glorious day into an utterly dark one.

Black Saturday

"Chief of Police Braisby was the first to spot Karauna. Karauna wore his felt hat. Leading the Vaimoso group and beating a bass drum, he must have stood out like a flashing neon light.

"At a junction near the police station, Machine Gunner Waterson spotted him too. 'That's Karauna with the felt hat. Get him!' he instructed an officer named Fell, who quickly moved to arrest Karauna. That's when the beast roared.

"Samoans landed blows on Fell. A musician thrashed him with a cornet. Waterson and his men raced to Fell's assistance. Waterson drew his pistol and fired. The pistol jammed. More police officers dashed into the fray, opening fire. A hand-to-hand combat followed. Outnumbered, Waterson and his men retreated. At the station, Waterson grabbed a Lewis gun and fired over the crowd.

"In the heat of the fighting, Tamasese dashed forward
with a rolled-up umbrella calling, 'Peace, Samoa, peace.' A
bullet shredded his thigh and he tumbled forward. Three
men shielded him. Bullets riddled their bodies. Others
scampered for safety; some stumbling, others casting about
for rocks. One rock sent young police officer, Abraham, to
the ground. A blow ended his life.

"When all settled, Tamasese and others lay stretched on
the street, their garments stained red."

Finest Moment

Tama clamped a palm over his mouth to stifle a whimper. "I know," Papa said gently. "Tamasese was a man of peace who wanted only the best for Samoa. At the hospital, surrounded by friends, he spoke with calm resolve. He seldom gave in to bad anger. 'My blood has been spilled for Samoa,' he said. 'I am proud to give it. Do not dream of avenging it, as it was spilled in maintaining peace. If I die, peace must be maintained at any price.'

"Tamasese's heart weakened, then gave up."

Tama made no attempt to hide his tears. "Tamasese followed Jesus' example," he said, sniffling. "Jesus forgave people even as they mocked and nailed Him to a cross."

Papa nodded. "In fact, in an earlier meeting with *Mau* chiefs, Tamasese prayed Jesus' prayer, 'Father, forgive them for they know not what they do.'"

Wiping a cheek with his sleeve, Tama leaned forward. "So, Papa, did Tamasese's peaceful act make our Samoa a Christian nation?"

"A nation is not Christian because a founding father was Christian. A Christian nation is known by its form of government. The answer is also in Samoa's Constitution. Is it founded on God's principles or man's principles? That has been the struggle since Adam disobeyed God and followed

his own will. But even in man's disobedience, God controls everything—even the evil and bad conducts of men."

Tama nodded, absorbing the lesson. "I should work on my bad anger, eh Papa?"

"*Ioe!* Yes," Papa winked, softening the mood. "The Bible says, 'Walk in wisdom toward outsiders, making the best use of the time.' And now that you're cooled off, what do you say to a Pineapple Smoothie?"

Tama beamed from ear to ear. "I say it's a perfect ending to a perfect story."

Author's Note

In America, men have passed laws that leave out God. They have replaced or altered Christian principles to fit man's desires. The result is increased lawlessness, selfishness, cruelty and violence. Many feel America is no longer a Christian nation. But was it ever one?

Some historians believe a Christian nation is known by its form of government, and whether or not its constitution is based on God's principles. That made me look up Samoa's constitution. I love Samoa. It is the country of my heritage.

In Samoa's constitution, I read *"...the Leaders of Samoa have declared that Samoa should be an Independent State based on Christian principles and Samoan custom and traditions...."* The words "Samoan custom and traditions" trouble me. We know customs and traditions change all the time—like shifting sand. And shifting sand is not a good foundation for anything. But God's Word is because it never changes to accommodate man's wicked desires.

Tupua Tamasese Lealofi III's story inspired me to write *Peace, Samoa, Peace.* Though Tamasese lived a short life (28 years), he tried to live it based on God's Word. I pray Samoa does not abandon Tamasese's beautiful example. When a nation follows God, the psalmist says: "Blessed is the nation whose God is Yahweh, the people whom He has chosen for His own inheritance" (Legacy Standard Bible).

www.ingramcontent.com/pod-product-compliance
Lightning Source LLC
Chambersburg PA
CBHW042118030726
47599CB00002B/259